D0467721

THE INFINITE
TULIP

HAROLD FEINSTEIN

BULFINCH PRESS

AOL TIME WARNER BOOK GROUP · BOSTON · NEW YORK · LONDON

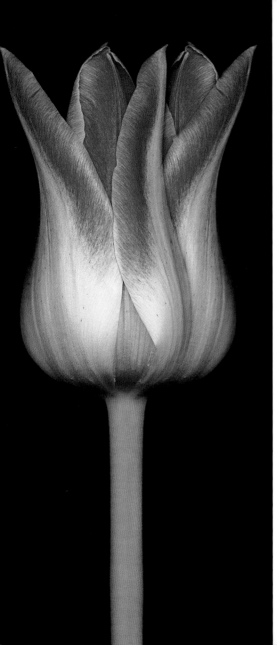

For Sarah, Shaler, Adam, and Gjon

ACKNOWLEDGMENTS

I wish to thank the following people: Jo-Anne S. Ohms of John Scheepers and Van Engelen for her generous advice about tulips; Lance Hidy for his strong design and perpetual input in the editing; Cindia Sanford, whose personal involvement with and love of flowers has been a continuous inspiration; Cherie Beaumont for her organizational support.

I also want to thank Jill Cohen, publisher, and Michael Sand, editor, at Bulfinch for their enthusiastic efforts on behalf of this book.

My wife and soulmate, Judith, for her warmth, wisdom, and love.

Lastly, I want to thank Fabia Barsic-Ochoa and Dan Steinhardt of Epson America, whose printers and scanners made this project feasible. HF

First Edition
ISBN 0-8212-2874-9
Library of Congress Control Number 2003112726

Bulfinch Press is a division of AOL Time Warner Book Group.

Design by Lance Hidy
PRINTED IN ITALY

PAGE ONE: PRINCESS IRENE
FRONTISPIECE: SPLENDORA
LEFT: ELEGANT LADY

THE INFINITE TULIP

In teaching photography, my basic instruction is "When your mouth drops open, click the shutter!"

When I was photographing the extraordinary variety of tulips, with my mouth dropping open almost continuously, the phrase "the infinite tulip" burst from my mouth.

And so the title of this book was born.

Feathery petals, graceful stems with leaves of a dancer, colors from chrome yellow to the whitest of white – such was the beauty, it was almost unbearable. Were it not for the medium of photography, it would have been thus for me. When I am asked about my technique, I reply, "A prayer"–

A prayer of gratitude:
gratitude for the beautiful flowers, and
gratitude for the eyes to see them with.

FRINGED CARNIVAL

SALMON PARROT

FRINGED FLAIR

YELLOW PARROT

WIROSA

AVIGNON

OVERLEAF

FANCY FRILLS

DUTCH FAIR

RED WHITE PARROT

PASSIONALE

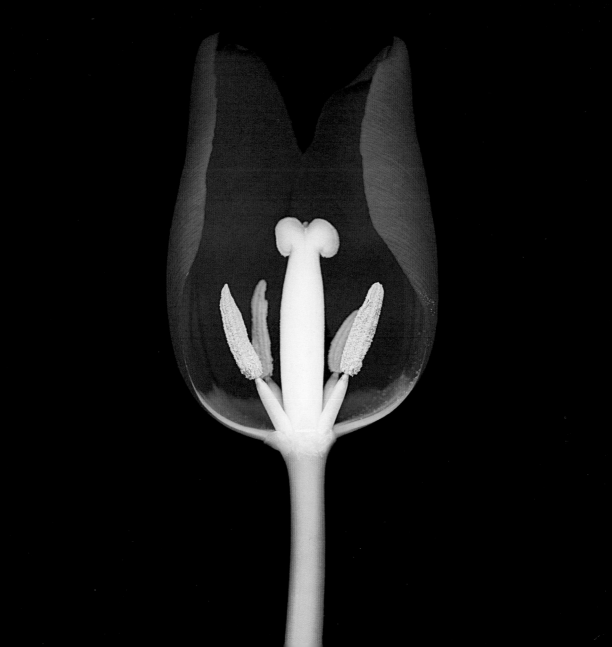

PINK BOUQUET

SPRING GREEN

ARABIAN MYSTERY

O'HARA TRIUMPH TULIP

WEBER'S PARROT

PARADISE

BLUSHING BEAUTY

SPRING GREEN

ROCOCO PARROT

SPRING GREEN

PURISSIM PARROT

HYBRID DREAM

SALMON PARROT

DARWIN HYBRID

RED WHITE PARROTS

DUTCH FAIR

FRINGED PARROT

LEEN VAN DER MARK

DOUBLE CIRCUS PARROT

STRIPED BELLONA

BEAU MONDE

FAMILY CLUSTER

CHINA PARROT

GREEN WAVE PARROT

OPEN DREAM

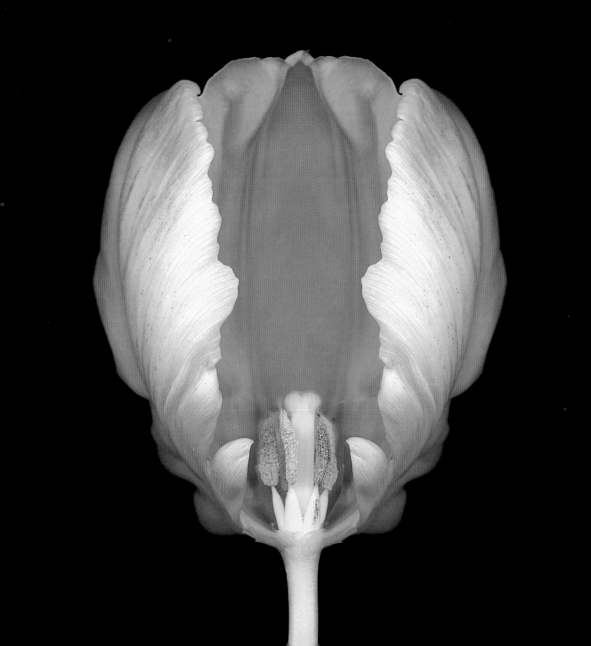

GAVOTTA

FLAMING PARROT

GREEN WAVE

PRESIDENT KENNEDY

FLAMING PARROT

ESTHER

APRICOT PARROT

PARADISE

FLAMING PARROT

YELLOW SMILE

QUEEN

ARABIAN MYSTERY

TULIPA ELITE

PARROT TULIP HYBRID

PARROT TULIP BOUQUET

ORANGE PROMINENCE

OVERLEAF

APRICOT PARROT

CAPE COD PARROT